# NECK OF THE WOODS

# NECK OF THE WOODS

AMY WOOLARD

Alice James Books
Farmington, Maine
www.alicejamesbooks.org

10 9 8 7 6 5 4 3 2 1

Alice James Books are published by Alice James Poetry Cooperative, Inc., an affiliate of the University of Maine at Farmington.

Alice James Books
114 Prescott Street
Farmington, ME 04938
www.alicejamesbooks.org

Library of Congress Cataloging-in-Publication Data

Names: Woolard, Amy, 1973- author.
Title: Neck of the woods / Amy Woolard.
Description: Farmington : Alice James Books, 2020.
Identifiers: LCCN 2019036014 (print) | LCCN 2019036015 (ebook) | ISBN
    9781948579070 (paperback) | ISBN 9781948579636 (ebook)
Subjects: LCGFT: Poetry.
Classification: LCC PS3623.O7124 (print) | LCC PS3623.O7124 (ebook) | DDC
    811/.6--dc23
LC record available at https://lccn.loc.gov/2019036014
LC ebook record available at https://lccn.loc.gov/2019036015

Alice James Books gratefully acknowledges support from individual donors, private foundations, the University of Maine at Farmington, the National Endowment for the Arts, and the Amazon Literary Partnership.

Cover art: Lori Nix

# CONTENTS

III

IV

# ACKNOWLEDGMENTS

Grateful acknowledgment is made to the editors & staff of the publications in which these poems have appeared:

*Bennington Review:*   "Reverse: A Fairy Tale"
                       "What I Told The Cops"

*Boston Review:*   "We Do Not Have Any Openings
                   At This Time"

*The Brooklyn Quarterly:*   "Ain't No Party"
                            "Gods Gone Wild" "Leading"
                            "Spoiler [It ends with the house
                            in the sky...]"

*Colorado Review:*   "Everyone Assumes The Animals
                     All Know Each Other"

*Court Green:*   "A Place Where There Isn't
                 Any Trouble"

*crazyhorse:*   "The Blueprint"

*failbetter:*   "On The Most Terrifying Character
                In The Wizard Of Oz"
                "We Will Have Wanted To Have"

Fence:                        "A Girl Keeps Getting Older;
                               The Looking Glass
                               Stays The Same Age"

Guernica:                     "Neck Of The Woods"

Gulf Coast:                   "After The Girl"

Indiana Review:               "The Girl Next Door To The Girl
                                  Next Door"
                               "In Ground We Trust"

The Journal:                  "Straw Man"

The Massachusetts Review:     "After The Witch"

The New Yorker:               "Spoiler [Was born a shamble.]"

Phoebe:                       "The Blonde Path"

Ploughshares:                 "How To Walk Backwards Into A
                                  Black & White House"

Puerto del Sol:               "The Housewarming"
                               "We've Been Gone Such A Long
                                  Time & We Feel So Messy"

Smartish Pace:                "Girl Gets Sick of Rose"

TriQuarterly:                 "Things Go South"
                               "While Away"

*Tupelo Quarterly*:                    "Echolalia"

*Virginia Quarterly Review*:           "An Engine That Won't"
                                       "Place Like Home"
                                       "What She Didn't Leave"
                                       "Get Lost"
                                       "Mise En Place"

"Girl Gets Sick Of Rose" also appeared in *Best New Poets 2013: 50 Poems from Emerging Writers*, edited by Brenda Shaughnessy.

"A Place Where There Isn't Any Trouble" also appeared in *Best New Poets 2015: 50 Poems from Emerging Writers*, edited by Tracy K. Smith.

"Mise En Place" also appeared in *Best New Poets 2018: 50 Poems from Emerging Writers*, edited by Kyle Dargan.

"After The Girl" also appeared on *Verse Daily*.

I'm incredibly grateful to everyone at Alice James Books for bringing this book to life. I'm also so thankful to the National Endowment for the Arts & Vermont Studio Center for generously providing resources, time, & space to make it happen.

I am so fortunate to have had incredible teachers along the way: Rita Dove, Greg Orr, Larry Levis, Jorie Graham, C.D. Wright, Forrest Gander, Jim Galvin, Donald Justice—& an especial, immeasurable amount of gratitude to Charles Wright, my Poetry Dad. What a constellation you all make.

I'm fiercely lucky that my favorite writers & editors & artists also happen to be my dear friends. Heather Derr-Smith, Deb Heishman,

Dahlia Lithwick, Sally Mann, Michael Jay McClure, Doug Powell, Mary Szybist, Allison Wright, Jane Yeh: thank you each & all for lending your absolute & particular grace to me.

Sam Baker, Jay Chowdhry, Jonathan Graham, Reggie Jackson, & Sarah Jackson: I reckon you've been in my speed-dial since I first had a phone number, & I can only hope you always will be. I love you all.

To the Professor: We'll go down this road 'til it turns from color to black & white.

To my home of Charlottesville—all my restaurant family, all the drummers & songwriters & bartenders & artists & parking lot attendants, & all the lawyers & organizers & activists—thank you for wilding me into all my selves.

First, last, & forever: unending love & gratitude for my family: Harry Roberts, Meg & Jim Woolard, Jennifer Woolard & Will Jarvis, Jamie Woolard & Gillian White, & Nate, Lucy, Henry, & Lilah—& all the dogs (& two cats) I've cared for along the way. It's all for & because of you.

for Rebecca & me

# THE HOUSEWARMING

It started before the first guests began arriving, before the three-hour tapers began melting their last hour, before the chocolates & gin, before the swarms of bees began making their way north, & the mice began stealing clumps of hair from your brushes, before the nightmares of your father's death, & once it started, *& you knew it would,* you could hear its click like a mechanical valve in the heart, feel it lean into you like your tongue curled in your mouth, pressing like the new book under your jacket as you head out into the downpour, tight in the gut as the flame-tipped arrow before it's sprung to set the floating coffin ablaze, *thief, thief,* hand on the back of the neck, hand on the poisoned apple, as if safety were a place we could be pulled to.

I

# SPOILER

It ends with the house in the sky
Slamming back onto its acreage. The girl

Inside is not the same girl who lived there in
The beginning—*hide the pieces, where they may be found.*

The wind begins to die down. Her pickup truck's gone
Feral in the tall grass. It is awful hot. *It's ok, you're still*

*An animal*, she says to herself. Animals are darned
With their past lives. The front porch can't help

But laugh at such a rookie mistake, claps
Its door, makes its ends meet. Either end

Of the truck's bench seat could prop her up—&
Home is just where you park yourself, right? Home is

Wherever you land. Hide your eyes if you have to,
Put your hand to your gut like a spoon, a belt.

But soon, you know you'll bring yourself
To look for her, to place her at the scene.

Whatever a girl gone leaves behind becomes
*Haunting.* If she returns, it is a *blessing.*

What would do it any justice? What I can
Tell you is: no one is left hanging.

# THE BLONDE PATH

When I visit hell I carry a paper girl with me
As currency. Black minidress with white tabs
That fold over her shoulders.

A demolition after my own heart.

The hostess searches my bag at the door.
She confiscates my red marker,
My syringe filled with mortar & bricks,
& threatens to banish me if I am heard
Listing the names of flowers.

She shows me to a table where my past lover
Sits by himself. His eyes are shifty & seductive
As spring flowers. He is the one who taught me
Always to have a second rasp of voice
Behind my voice. I am grateful.

My eyes are accurate as green canoes.

He tells me stories of explorers
In undersea caves. The ones that go for miles.

Each time he touches me,
The sky drops fifty feet. I tell him
The three main ways I don't want to die.
I tell him I'd like to live in a lighthouse.
He doesn't seem to know when I'm lying.
He takes a cigarette without asking, & asks
Where my better half is.

It will not break me.

Forsythia, oncidium, daisy, a light tingle
On my shoulders as if I were just out of reach
Of an invisible whip's crack.

*Sweetheart*: a miniature of the original, as in roses.

Whisper *forget-me-not* & see where it gets you.

You don't know if you're coming or going.

When I come to you it will be
From a great distance & it will be likely
That I unwind a spool of wire
Behind me, somewhere connected to something
I planted in my sleep.

I've postponed spring for now
& look forward to the summer.
I see the bride in everyone.
Time-lapse clouds roll overhead.

I make lists just to get the feel for
Crossing things off.

Inject a house into the horizon, inject a secret
Passage, a secret room, a waterwheel
Of jealousies attached to the house,
A fire far in the backyard, large enough
So the nearing boats will have to choose.

Something is wrong.
In the end, aren't there always stars?
What is missing is the porch.

# A PLACE WHERE THERE
# ISN'T ANY TROUBLE

Girl walks into a house & comes out running. Girl runs down

A neighborhood street & a pickup rolls up beside her. Storm's

Coming. Aunt says Girl you know there're monsters out there

& you never know. Aunt says Sugar this storm'll run roughshod

Over the dirt you call childhood, farm & storm spread so wide they

Each get a name. Whiskey rolls down her throat & lights the farm

On fire. Aunt says Girl there're monsters in this world you'll call

Friends in the next, storms that'll write your name in the sky,

Clouds that roll up & announce you like a choir. A fire don't

Chase but it catches. The bells of the neighborhood church keep

Pealing on without you & do not call you home. Around here,

*Ugly* ain't a name for the way somebody looks, but how she talks or

Talks back. *Rotten* isn't just for apples; it's for how she acts. Girl walks

Into the woods & comes out a monster. Storm kicks up beside her.

Mongrel paces just behind her footfall. There're farms in this world,

But Girl & Mongrel are headed to the next. Around here, strip

Where a field meets the woods is called *The Invitation*. Stray piece

Of straw on her skirt like an unlit match. Stray light splintering

Through the branches like tangled hair. Oh & she is lit

With whiskey now. Now a fugue settles over the trees.

Now a path undresses itself in front of her, fingers her

Forward. On the other side of an invitation, somebody's always

Cooking up something. Trouble is a dish. A prayer: *Fill my plate*

*With sugared apples. Fill my heart with discipline.* Mongrel cases

Any new body might stand in her way. If you can't beat them,

Join them, the farm calls. If you can't join them, let them

Walk you to your truck but when it's time to go, it's time to go,

The bells peal. Girl peels off her Sunday skirt like a bell gone

Soft. An invitation is just another line to be crossed, after all,

All of it rinsed with a light, salted. Girl leaves the farm lit

Behind her, but takes the path with her when she goes,

Wherever she goes, pretty as you please. Full of sugared

Breath to waste on the crook of the next one's neck. The dirt

I could dish, thinks Mongrel, *I'm the one she'll miss the most.*

Well, shoot. Somebody got to be the one who stands burning

On the porch, waves Aunt, & somebody got to be the one to get lost.

# LEADING

The question suggests to the witness the answer the examining party desires. *You were waiting for me out on the porch? Stayed out there even when the storm kicked up?* The girl has arranged her dolls in order of their intelligence. The ones whose eyes can open & close are either first or last in line. Turkey vultures stutter up above, lashes caked with mascara. The scent of something coming. *You don't think you might've been mistaken.*

Of course things begin to go south just before supper. Salted watermelon on a plate in the kitchen. White seeds like coughed-up aspirin some throat refused. The sky breathes in, the opposite of a sigh. The fat rain comes as far as the front steps & gives its best advice: ask questions first; ask forgiveness later. All the dumb flowers stay open anyway.

# GET LOST

When I hear that boy sing, I said, every other
Boy becomes a disappointment. Tiny wince

Like the sound of a beetle underfoot. *Sure it hurts*
*But it should hurt sometimes.* I think this is the part

Where the fiddle slips in beside me & tries for
The heart, a photo stuck in someone else's book.

Turns out, you can't even take the girl out
Of the South. A good porch is hard to leave,

& that's the truth. Gardenias & a hand-rolled smoke.
A fingerbone of moon tapping at the screen door. Who

You're looking for depends on who wants to know. You know,
I have a cotton dress & a closed-mouth smile for any occasion.

You went for your keys. I went to pull what I thought
Was a tangle out of my hair, but found a tiny braid

I reckon you must've made while I was sleeping. Nice try.
You can't kiss me & expect to leave a prayer like that behind.

Out here, some things are fixed with a hot shower, some
With a better lock on the door. When you see a girl propped

In her chair like a shotgun still warm, I think you know:
That's no riddle. Sun split open the morning like a tenpenny.

Pair of yard dogs cased your truck. Those two know what V-E-T spells,
You better believe it. Out here, where there's tires, there's dust.

When I hear that boy sing my skin tightens with sunburn & I start
Sleeping on top of the sheets, under a fan & beside no one. I use

The word sugar like a leash like I'm both the heat & the
Humidity & you're just idling with the windows down.

Here we go again, I all but say. Tell me something I
Don't know, says the truck, windshield smitten with insects.

## STRAW MAN

Want a little smoke in the alley. Want a little kiss in the

Cornfield. Am parched, papery as an old hive. Open

Your arms wide for me now, love; show me the nothing

That is surely up your sleeves. Here there is a single word

That means *the girl will come this way soon*. Here there is

A girl who will make you her favorite in the morning

Just to leave you at noon. Wake me into your arms,

Love; set yourself up for a fall, a fool. Figure that the

Distraction you provide is just someone's version of a

Golden rule. If I only had a brain that wasn't paid for.

Pour yourself into your work, dear—pull yourself together.

Cinch my love like a lit wick between your fingers. But

Remember: you get what you stay for. If country accident,

Then city conspiracy; if sweat on the small of the back, then

The wet feathers of a new-hatched bird. Fashion a proper

Fetish of my hair, the loose strands you find like indictment

All around you, the prop the actor needs to stay in character.

Tinker with your lines but hit your mark, the way shapes—

The lamp, the chair—emerge out of the dodgy dark like

Cartilage once our eyes adjust, love, once we while away

Our hours: you & your bed are cut from the same cloth.

# PLACE LIKE HOME

I was asked to show up with a sidedish. I made
A slaw of my longing. I had to keep it crisp. Nothing goes

Bad in a backyard, if you catch my drift. In a
Backyard everything is available like a catalog

World, viz.: I carried a plastic basket of fluffed
Clean clothes propped on one hip as if

A small, outdoor-fresh child. Time it takes
To smoke a 100, I'll've forgotten the second

Of three friends gone. Dry skin sky. Heartless jolt
Of a lawn mower kicking forward into gear. Wind

Punch at a pinned-up line of blue bedsheets so to
Tell us about What's Coming. Porch chimes aren't

As dumb as you think they are. Oh bright laundry:
I like it when my stomach feels starved

For home. Hands trolling the dirty
Dishwater for lost forks. Facts:

Straw is to heartless body as *I lied when I said I hope*
*I'll see you all again* is to *Come home.* I like a lot of you

Most of the time, but I got my favorites. Don't matter
Which bricked world I thought I was living in,

The dog had his name, at least. The scarecrow was only
Ever called *Scarecrow*. Wind swing a backyard gate

Left open so to tell us about What's Gone.
Heart is to lost laundry as—Q: What if

I don't need to borrow any more boys'
T-shirts for bed. What if I'm already stuffed.

Those were the days, though, I tell you what! The way
I made a sky-blue gingham of my teenage years...

Before sleep, I like to think about all those snaking roads, &
The band geeks not wearing their seatbelts, & the prom-

Fluffed girls like sugar roses on grocery
Store sheet cakes, floating up the ladders

Of small-town water towers to graffiti
Their triumphant *1989*, sloppy in the flashlight

Moon. Oh sugar roses, I didn't even want to say that
Part about the moon, but we're all going down together.

When I didn't know what to make, I made
Breakfast. Chimes are to *sorry* as the secondhand

Smell of gasoline is to a twelve-year-old
Saturday morning. I want

To buy all the trucks parked for sale
In all the front yards in Virginia.

# MISE EN PLACE

The peonies are popping! A fist that is also a kettle that is also
A pact petals made with whatever cabal of bees decides to stick

Around. Let's all us shake on it. Ah, these lungs of mine the perfect
Emergency orange of extension cord coil. All my breathing is

Indoor/outdoor. Just be yourself, so I open a tab & order a
Whiskey, non-artisanal rocks. My sweat equity pays for itself.

Shoot, it only took half a second for it to get unpaid-electric-bill
Quiet up in here. The longing's prix fixe. Naturally, the peonies bang

Their way into the room, demand a table by the window. The city's
Swans give away the weather. Step out of the pond & into

The mix, swans! Make tracks like hatched forkprints on
Uncooked dough. Half a life is achieving a gorgeous crisp

Tear of a sugar packet's corner. Half a life is reaching
Casually for a dog who—sad to say—'s been gone for months.

# ON THE MOST TERRIFYING
# CHARACTER IN THE WIZARD OF OZ

It's not the part where he tells you
He has no heart. It's not when he

Tells you how much he wants one,
How everything until just now has been

Frozen for him in time, how the trees all
Seem so sour, & territorial, all while he hefts

That gleaming axe. It's not his silver tongue
Or how the tears fell like clockwork, then

Sawdust. It's not how he so casually walked off
The job that day, knowing he would follow

You anywhere. If only someone had thought
To change the music just as you asked him

To join you, a theremin, or some low-octave piano.
If only you hadn't run after so much disaster.

It's one kind of weapon to be able to tell a girl
A story; it's another kind to be able to walk her

Home. It's not even the way he tried to breathe
Those flowers deep into his tin lungs just so he could

Sleep beside you, dreaming of how his ticking
Heart would be the alarm that wakes you,

How his creaking arms would be the ones
To build you a house that stayed put.

It's the way he looks at you, the way he thinks
He's loved you since before you even first

Arrived here in front of him, hungry for
Apples that weren't even his to give you.

# NECK OF THE WOODS

Filthy as 12-bar, filthy as a stuttering key in the hazy
Door lock at 4 a.m. Filthy as *I don't know what it means to love*

*You.* Out in the country there's no fence to speak of—there's just
The blonde path, wide enough for a truck, a truck wide enough

For two bodies to ride restlessly beside one another without
Ever touching. There's no fence to speak of, just various dusks &

I'm in love with the dust that kicks up—I'm in love with what
A dirt road does to a truck. There's no *edge of the woods*—there's just

The blonde path stretching out of the dark green like a
Leg bone, a radio dial catching a hit of station before

Moving on past into the static. Two girls ride ruthlessly
Beside one another—one filthy as a story, the other filthy

As a storyteller. One girl might leave a trail of crumbs
Behind her. One might leave a line of poured-out gasoline.

Old evening air the way warm soda tastes like a hangover,
A long drive in July. *I got plenty of time. You got light in your eyes.*

It's all the middle of nowhere. When the music stops, everybody
Scatters, even the light—an embarrassment of a sunset, really, &

Why even talk about the stars as if we still care about them
In the off-hours, when we're not confessing to the dead?

These girls *wore* each other, is what I mean. Passed out in
Each other's shoes, passed the ends of sentences from one to

The other like taking belts of whiskey out the bottle. One
Night one girl waves goodbye to the other & the empty fifth

She leaves in my hand is where the story turns dark, is where
I stick myself against the story flush as a wheat-paste poster,

Contact-printing my body back onto itself, a decade delayed. Love,
This is where the joke begins: one girl's gotten gone. Her brother

Walks into a bar to deliver the punch line, & the other girl doubles
Over—*an inside job*. See, you got to be able to fall, for there to be

An edge—see the bar in waves, the doubled stars in waves, all just
Frosting on a cold cake. Both girls breathless in their own bodies now.

Now, it's a ruthless thing, to know what's about to happen to
Someone who does not know what's about to happen. One girl might

See years go by in waves of roadside signs, a trail of vein rise up
On the back of her hand before it begins to wind down the twin

Bones of her forearm. Two girls trailed each other, delivered one
Another from one year to the next, twinned until they wound down

To just one night. One girl might leave a line of salt in the dirt,
One a flush of dust, sifted into a river. What is there left to leave

When there's no body to speak of? This is where the storyteller
Begins: I am trying to know what it means to love anyone

Else the way I meant to love her, the way a sweet tooth
Loves salt. Sugar, I used to know this place like the back

Of my papery hand. Now there's just the blonde past,
A river oversaturated with roses & ash, a back way

Home, a way back to what there ever is to leave behind.
I am trying. The smell of fresh pine, the small task of rain

On a windshield, a drift like the bow of a single fiddle
Drawing itself across my collarbone, my lungs sinking & rising

Slow like sloppy keys in a deep octave, my heart resting dark
Like a gun in a glovebox whenever I might need to lean for it.

I've paid some hush money to the unpaved path, the paved-
Over past, plucked up the door lock & parked two loose cigarettes

In the useless tapedeck, then that small piece of quiet—after the click
Of the ignition but before the radio cuts on, the quarterglass

Coaxing in the scalene country air, yellowing its passengerless slant
Over half the truck's bench seat, the angles catching nobody, missing it all

—What any girl with half a mind wanders out this way for, to take
As much of it in over & over & sure enough breathe it all the way out.

II

# SPOILER

Where there were fresh brides, now there run
Other women's children, trails of unfinished

Sentences, bright as morning blood from my gums.
None of it good fun. Where there was the wet & quick

Burn of the ear-piercing gun, now there swipes the tire-skid
Grey swatch of skin under each eye, the tiniest flagless

Terrain, where longing takes root, makes good. O first
Face you fiend to see when you wake—leave me

For the way the weight of my head makes your arm fall
Asleep, for the state of undress darkening your floor, the spill &

Slip of myself I pour out a little for her—up & dirty—
Each lost year that waits for us. *We love a thing we cannot*

*Know.* A decade left laid out for me like a salt lick, attractive,
The way nobody gets what she wants is attractive, the way

Desire wicks away memory from this skin & sends it—where.
Time was, you couldn't tell where I was headed by

The way I was put together, other women's clothes on
The line, other numb in my lungs like bees or badlessness

Or boredom. Where does a girl leave her footprint when she's
Already home? I mean, where can a girl go around here to spend

A little salt. Throw a little weight of the world around, wait
Up for late night, when I'm beside myself with if & how to

Tell it, when who's to say I'm even up for this. Story goes,
I just had to get gone, slip solo out the house for a spell, roll

My love around, a cooked egg in its shell crackling under
My palm. Sweetheart, who's to say where the holes in this story

Fall. The way I was put back together, it's no wonder I fell
For the bricks beneath me, all spun up with what I could leave

An imprint of my lipstick on next, the hours so followable, so
Wet & quick, so nearly lickable & late, late, & the weight of

My head so sure I'd need to find that receipt in my pocket
In the morning. Said & done, it's no wonder we all stay so long.

# AFTER THE WITCH

Winter whiskered the air peculiar.
I was homesick. The house needs me,
I am convinced. It's laughable,
A girl left lying in the woods.

A list I could make would include:
Forest musk, the low fence,
One witch quick to coals,
Two naps in thicket.

I had a doll once.
When you laid her down, her eyes closed.

Each chocolate brick aligned in the chimney,
The yard zipped up by the low fence.
A list I could make would include:

Sugar-coated window, forest musk,
One witch bricked in the chimney,

& I let loose in the kitchen, aproned,

& I by morning blonde, & altogether sweet.

I know how to make myself.
The last kitten left lapping at the back door,
Pancakes tanning on the griddle. It's laughable.

I said I was homesick.

A list I would have made would include:
Winter, kitten at back door,
Girl left lying in woods.
When you lay her down, her eyes close.

# THE BLUEPRINT

If it isn't one room, it will be another,

When you find your way back, chalking
The walls, the better to lose yourself again

My dear, there will always be something
That cannot be described exactly

As a room: a stairwell, a closet, a porch
With the one light left lit for you, &

If it isn't in one room, it will be in another,
Curled up as a lost sonata, or a blueprint

For an entire town, its traffic bottlenecking
At the sight of you, how everything will seem the opposite

Of a hallway, it's all coming back to me now,
Like too many parentheses, tulips will crowd each other

& me, as if in mute love with you, the wind
Will end up narrowing where I can walk,

All over town, girls will fall in love

With starvation, *the sky—the sky—*

Get it through that thick heart of yours,
It will all dead end at my door:

Player pianos will rewind themselves without hesitation
Or remorse, secret passageways will reveal themselves

As simple bookshelves after all, I will see you
In no one's eyes, no one's architecture,

It will all just be one room after another.

# EVERYONE ASSUMES THE ANIMALS ALL KNOW EACH OTHER

Geese these days really need to work on their Vs.
Tornados need to slow their roll & keep their cones tight.

Don't get it twisted: the dogs are here to teach us how to lose
Something important. The bears know what's what. The ants just

Want it more than we do. The cats have reached consensus
On refusing to pull us out of fires. It's that old grift: if

You love someone, leave them be. So they've sent in the magpie
To work us undercover. It's important to have someone

On the inside. A wasp would be too obvious, nervously
Banging itself against each glazed windowpane like an amateur.

A roach would just bring up all the old nightmares, skittering
Across the floor like a cigarette cherry thrown out a car window

Onto the dark interstate. But a magpie is our ultimate prize:
A thief who doesn't need us but chooses us anyway—&

All the while, he's picked up on all our tells,
Tucked certain of our favorite words into his beak,

Smuggling them out for constructing his next nest until
We're left with only our own small commands: Sit, stay,

Speak until we lie down together. The magpie, without telling
Us in so many words, will be the one pulling our strings when

We play favorites with the ones we know we cannot keep &
The ones we try to replace: the collarless puppies falling all

Over each other like fountain water, tussling while we lie
In wait for the moment they become motherless.

# HOW TO WALK BACKWARDS INTO A BLACK & WHITE HOUSE

Oak branches shuffling slow amends in the sorry wind, as if trying to push
A large gift into your arms. Step back into your dusty boots, love, left &

Right then, creased like fruits gone to rot. Filling up an outline of myself,
Is all. You're the reason here they call a mouth a trap. Everybody's safest

When a trap's shut, except one. Bless your fool heart, is what I mean.
The room upstairs has your bag in it, looks out on the backyard, opens

Onto the sleeping porch. Oh, you can talk to the dead, but you can't
Make them drink. The neighborhood bells peal & repeal their supper

Swoon song: Bless the hound, the lightning bug, the propane tank
Steeped in weeds. The driveway is there because the truck says so.

The Rappahannock's just a papercut, a cowlick. The things you keep
Crying to me through the window screen: *The icebox door's wide*

*Open. A hornet nest's tucked up in a corner just over your bed.*
The things I know how to fix. No one told me to find this place

Beautiful—I grew up out of it like a blue hydrangea out of the dead
Of winter. I feel my age when I rub my front teeth. You think I can

Just waltz back in there? A tousle in my lungs when I picture you
Behind me, love, a day-moth staking out the porch bulb. *Sitting perched*

*On front steps* is Southern for *longing*, the evening Juned with light &
Sweat & a cold, cold can of beer. Wrap your arms around me.

Wrap your truck around me. A photograph grows older the more
You look at it. A front door here is always two doors & each is

A different answer to a knock—both have to say *come in*, but one
Can say *come closer*. Supper's growing colder, so bow your head:

Bless the unsifted flour in its bin & bless it sifted into the biscuits.
Bless the coated rolling pin. Bless your floured palms. My love

I give to you like a Dixie cup in the middle of the night. What cuts
Through this place, what rises isn't water, but ain't mud neither.

I've got the whole world in my fists. I've got the whole
Wide world. Your children weren't meant to be my children.

# WHILE AWAY

When the satellite signal berserks, the conversations
Begin. Today's devotional: Windex scattershot, ecstatic

Gasp of the punctured cat food tin. It seems everything
Within earshot has something to say. The linoleum unpeels

Itself, an obscene gesture clearly meant for the wood
Floor gloating in the hallway, a throat choked with

Orchid & its own wool tongue. The orange peels & cayenne
Drop a dime on the cat. The pink of the disposable razor ignites

An unwinnable debate with the pangs of pocketchange
Loose in the dryer. The shower curtain remembers

Then forgets to hide the claw feet, then chucks its rings
Into the tub like breadcrumbs, like laughter.

Broil is the oven's only talent. It's silk when I slip
My hands into that heat, like testing a stocking for holes.

Well what do you expect when you give a house a name?
Let's review: first, I am redundant with bleach. Next,

The gutters are drunk again. Finally, even the wildlife
Know better than to put a lock on something

Made of glass. When my kiss turns
Lemon-fresh, I'll know to wipe it clean.

# GIRL GETS SICK OF ROSE

When I asked for a pencil, they gave me a rattle.
When I asked for a hammer, they gave me a kiss.
All mongrel, no matter, I'll stay out past dinner;
I've stolen the answers to all of their tests.

I've given up sweets, their ridiculous shapes,
Their instructions on which ones have cherries.
Everything under the sun is lukewarm;
The poppies are blooming with worry.

When they gave me a map, I thought they were done,
I thought I could take off my dress.
They told me one town was as good as another;
Sent me packing, all fiddle, no case.

Each cul-de-sac greyed like a cooled blown bulb.
All dashboard, all driver, all sky & no cake,
Each neighborhood gatehouse, a live empty socket.
When they asked for my ticket, I gave them a wink.

The instructions all listed Step One as Repeat,
The poppies were planted in rows at the park.
I lived on a circle, then moved onto a square,
Then wandered back into the kitchen half-drunk.

The screen door, the scrim, the latch, the last word.
The glass throats of each vase open wide.
A house is the largest headstone we make;
We keep walking, grateful, inside.

# ECHOLALIA

[Dorothy, *Wicked Witch of the East*]

This is the scene where I'm supposed to want to go home.
*Sometimes your voice is like getting stitches & sometimes it's like getting stitches removed.*

The distance between my lungs & my house is the difference between yellow & gold.
*What we see in black & white is authentic; what we see in color is true.*

Storm keeps coming the way Aunt kneads dough scraps until the last biscuit is cut.
*When the heart is a glass souvenir from a landscape you once road-tripped.*

The barn is raised & the barn is razed—a natural disaster, is the story I'm told.
*When the heart is a snow globe of the Dust Bowl, shaken.*

Aunt says: Swallow an orange seed & a tree will sprout in your stomach.
*Eat to its core an apple a day & still in the end worms will wend into your lungs.*

I stash all my love for you in my shins, is why I wear kneesocks.
*Even the mosquitos make a beeline for your ankles straight away.*

What do you call a girl who doesn't come when she's called?
*A first love is just an animal who either waits too long or doesn't wait long enough.*


Do you know what it's taken for me to even miss you at all?
*People who seem to just fall off the earth of your face.*


Poppies like a field of cigarette burns.
*When your friends are flammable, you quit smoking.*

# WE'VE BEEN GONE SUCH A LONG TIME
# & WE FEEL SO MESSY

We ask where are we & then we are
In a quandary. We feel our way
Around—the room, it's dark with surprise—
We enter & we light it. Slick
& curving close to the face
Like hairstyles of the '20s.

*We plume the house with us.* Our sleep thinks

We can save people. We look at
The lamps & their bulbs begin unscrewing. The music
Begins. We try to introduce ourselves & people
Call us a one-trick match.

We got a bad crush. He cuts us
Strings of paper dolls. One to one, they blacken they
Pickpocket each other's pink. We look out
At the stars & they wince. Like a smoke detector
Our sleep keeps its one red eye on us.

The hostess steps out for more ice
& around the room things begin
To come up missing:

Where we are, everyone looks at us—we are told
We don't have to go home

But we can't stay here. Improperly kissed
We are messy with the crush. We crush
Together like violet like spring bulbs.
We piece things together & our eyes
Widen. Our sleep says Do you always
Burn holes through people like that?

# WHITE KNUCKLE

Age-old: a girl—>a fall—>
A different set of girl. Once &

Future serifed with some grief or
Other. Thrown for a loop as a way

Of saying you're *storied*. Alice, e.g.,
Takes a real spill, & not for nothing.

A body does not cooperatively adjust
To its borders, an arm drawn hanging

Out a window, captioned as Queen
Or Thief, depending on its sleight.

A modern tale: a girl slips away but
Does not fall, or fell but only fell as far

As her neck's last angle. Hang on: but how
To chalk an outline of the air around her;

The officials were lost. The next day was
Frisky without her. That was the morning

I stopped placing myself in anyone other's
Hands. No cake, no drink, no broth could be

Brought, to coax the heal or give best
Gesture to it. A girl—>a grip. No pressure

Point a palm would know to resize, unknot.
Rest assured, love: *There will be nonsense in it.*

A backlog of blackbirds trafficking in *I*
*Told you so.* She was mean, & mine, &

Nicked lousy in her peripheral, how
Oncidium blossoms plot close, wasps

Tucked into a rented house's gutter.
Professionally speaking, I spoke it to

No one. All others else, not so much
Fell for them as fell against them.

I stopped. I hung on. The telltale:
My hands' jaws, my best guesses.

# SOMETHING AWFUL

Grief says: *First answer, best answer.* Ave gardenia, full of haste, my love
Backlit like a silent letter, a quiet car blurred black, riding backwards-

Facing towards Virginia, my ulcered undertongue brickled & still.

And still, Gut says: *First anger, best anger.* The wine is skunked & she & I
Down it. A buckshot of starlings against the grey—I figure it for seasoning &

Shake it flaking from my hair. It's spring & there's nothing good

To eat. Twice now I've asked the weather to shove off & still its pang
Persists. I'm sorry the way a plastic cup sweats. Even when the service left

Something to be desired, I pooled my tips. I've tried polite. My love pools & I

Finger it until I've swiped it wider, left it on the table. Until it sops
Into my wrist holding it down. I hold it down for her & anyone else

Who wants to leave before it's time. I've come to know when

It tastes like mine. I have been a country drunk & I have been
An apparatchik of plate glass. I got it in my sights. I tried to leave

That town an exit wound. I tried to carry her bags, but she insisted.

III

# SPOILER

I've likely told you too much already. What was found: a little routine
Metal, the feel of a man's watch on his wrist. The steel of it & the wrist

In my hand. The cuss of evening light. Whiskey moves through me like
It's checking me for ticks. My love rises, irises up in low oxygen.

We made a skill of missing each other, going dark too early. The radio
Silence was gold. Real talk: when all you have is a breath, everything bends

Like a rib. The porchlight lit & relit itself, developed unrequited  feelings
For the eaves. No one needs give me permission: first find tracks

In the mud, then the boots that sank them. What's seen in a
Window—> seen in a river just as well. I stationed myself,

Flat-backed in the crouch against the house, under the jargon
Of the sill. Truth be told, I was secreted beneath you. Then

There to the waterline in the time it takes your spoon of sugar
To commute from cellar to cup. Sink all the spare keys &

Vanish before your double-take turns. The urge of us comes late
To the game, blends unfreaked into the stand of trees, takes its peek.

Between you & me: there is no one thing that designed this, save what
Ever here or above made the fish that looks like sand when still.

The moth was made to look like a leaf. The bark was supposed to
Sound like trouble, but in that ever, all I heard was *Closer come closer*.

# FIRST MYSTERY

*"This is the first mystery I've solved alone," she thought.*

Overschooled townie is my business
Model. Revised myself fresh from

The old days, added sugar, succor, side-eye,
A girl's best friend. Listen here, I'm not above

Scaring up a little action. I mean, I'm the one
Who wears the plans in this family. Miss me

With the way I match that black truck, terrific
How I light it up: single-engine boys, impure

Thoughts dreaming off their bodies
Like gasoline fumes. I'll pull on one

Of my curls if I want to remember
Your name—it will be our signal. Oh I love to

Make time with all you haters; you know a clock
Can't ever keep a secret longer than an hour.

# AN ENGINE THAT WON'T

The town, my dear, is closing down: dead-
Bolts slipping into their sleeves, cicadas insisting

Like so many typewriters, drunk girls sleeping
In their shoes. Without you, the house begs

For disaster, love: extension cord nest, dismantled
Smoke detector. Something ticking—not like a bomb:

Like a gas burner trying to light, an engine that won't
Turn over. Turn over

The pillow & the stain vanishes. Tuck the blanket up around
It & the body appears. Anything can look like a person

From the right distance. Anything can take off
Like a house on fire. The kind of light that gets you

Out of bed in the morning. Since April I've had one foot
In someone else's grave, a drunk girl who left me

Her shoes. The way she would move through a party
Like cursive, a car passing through the underlit dark, gleaming

Like the eye of a cooked fish. What she didn't leave was a note.
What I mean is: what a cliffhanger. But wait, this is no time

To excuse yourself, dear: this is no time for a smoke, though
We're all a little hot under the collar these days. I mean, these days

If it isn't the screenless open windows, it's the chipped lips
Of the snifters, the splintered floorboards under your bare feet,

The hundreds of electrical wires, just humming under the plaster,
Just nearly bursting with the same sweet secret as ever—*Press*

*Your ear to the wall & hold your breath.* It's the absolute longing
The hair dryer feels for the bathroom spigot, & the ochre

Lungswell of water stain on the bedroom ceiling, there above
The pillow line. A blown bulb that crumbles in the unscrewing.

Sometimes two things appear so identical, you have to repeat
To yourself: *The dead battery is in my right hand; the replacement battery*

*Is in my left.* Dead, right. Replacement, left. But still you forget &
Spend good gotdamns you don't have to give switching one

For the other & back again: a jigsaw puzzle where all the pieces
Are just the same blue sky. As if the top two corners of anything

Could contain what there is in front of you to put together.
*It had to be you,* the radio wisecracks. *It had to be you.* The kind of lie

That gets you out of bed in the morning. The ceiling fan spins wildly
On its mismounted base, love, & you watch it like a wasp loose

In the room. Loose in the room, a girl clumsies her whiskey glass &
Even the music stops to gasp at the shatter. How many other ways

Were there for her to excuse herself? No matter: it's all dying
Down now. It's curtains for this party, fading the way

An old typewriter's letters bleed into the page. What I mean
Is: the lights of a town seen from above, turning off

Just before sleep. Just before sleep is when
I found her, love: flip the switch & the body appears.

# THIRD MYSTERY

*It is possible to hold one's hands while being bound so as to slip the bonds later.*

Details begin to emerge like a welt on the head. The river begins just
Before you apprehend it. A hint of coolness in your voice. Like a welt

Overhead, the storm begins. As if safety were a place
You could swim for, a littered shore, an unlit porch, a hot-

Wired sunset—love, don't take this the wrong way, but nobody
Needs another dream sequence. Nobody sleeps it off. Bet your

Rock-bottom dollar the house won't care. Case the kitchen &
You'll find yourself there, chaired under an assumed name, cuffed

With hunger—breakfast snapping in the pan while you wait
To be served, puzzle over who cooked the books. In the bedroom,

Suitcases still as a safecracker's cheek, & in a blink, it all
Clicks. The downed tree across the path, the burner & the blocked

ID—the resemblance was nothing if not striking. At least you're able
To articulate what all good misanthropes long for: *Too bad I'm not twins.*

# WE DO NOT HAVE ANY OPENINGS
# AT THIS TIME

Not a one tells it this way, save me: the girl'd aimed to pull herself out
Of herself & skipped first to the lungs. It all fits; it all starts: a slim-

Jimmed door lock. A lick-threaded needle, fed through knotless. I mean,
What gives. Hold hard & each one/thing slips through the fingers. Can you

Tell I carry inside of me the imprint my truck left on a 5 a.m. deer? We looked
Each other dead in the eye for a slow second & then a warm smack like a failed

Marriage. A bruise tried to cross me off, but only met me halfway. All bodies
A workshop of what isn't anymore there. There's loss & there's talking

About loss, & one will stay immeasurable & one'll world-without-end be looking
For containers to fill. One eyes the highball & sees the past as half-empty, half-

Spilled. Sugar, I can tell you're onto me: I want you the way I want someone
Gone. Quick puff of day-moon just waiting to poke holes in my story. Half-mile

Through some trees to the nearest other. I'll risk any path so long as
I've got my dog walking point. Like any driven girl who meets a wolf along

The way, I've got my talking points. The mistake is trying the first house you
Come to, door parted open like a close mouth deciding not whether but when

To kiss. Once I come to, you ask me to set the table. When I say I believe I
Could tell you anything, you deadpan & hand me a map of love that unfolds

To the life-size of love itself. Each dish you place in front of me features
Some animal I worry has the kind of bones you're not supposed to swallow.

# A GIRL KEEPS GETTING OLDER; THE LOOKING GLASS STAYS THE SAME AGE

All morning the hornet banging against the glass.
Some kind of shelves where should have been a door.
Rumors of the celebrity returning to town, barely
Two words to rub together. A mouth's a kind of map.
Make no mistake about it. My arms are growing rounder.
I've got a kind of quiet; it's like I'm a circle, the way I walk.
Only two edges to rub together. It's like my arms aren't matching
Up. Some kind of rumor where should have been a hornet.
A cello returning like your body, two pianos back to back,
Curling into one another. Slow quick quick; stop quick quick.
It's like I'm holding someone, the way I waltz.
My face is drying up. It's like my mouth is sleeping.
The walls all arc around me. The shelves all hold their edges.
A cello's a kind of hornet. A body's a kind of door.
Some kind of celebrity banging against the glass.

# SIXTH MYSTERY

*She had become so engrossed with the spilled perfume that she had forgotten*
*about the pale young woman who occupied the opposite seat.*


I was looking for a way to walk into the mouth
Of an open question, to follow her signature scent
Until I found myself checkered with its loss.
I was looking for a way to set us an example,

To follow her scent into her last open question, to
Signal so everyone knew it was hard work, the work of her.
Looks like she found a way to be her own example,
To love the body of any water & not only its bight.

The signals she sent took work; not everyone knew it—
A perfect telltale drape in her skirt, a fold like a girl
The fainting shape of water, a body going dark at the bight.
I wanted to counterfeit her, to be honest. Pass her off as me,

Like a girl who tells her skirt its origin tale, a fabric
So checkered with its own loss, I couldn't find mine.
To be honest with her, I had to pass her off, & wanted to.
Look at my mouth: it's the only way I can walk into her.

# WHAT I TOLD THE COPS

I slept in a study & woke in a kitchen. Yes,
Every night from when I showed up. Showing up

Is half the battle & better ready than fed. So I can
Close the zipper on my skirt all the way, I hold my

Tongue. Sure, take a look around—you've all the fixings of
A confession: spinning wheel, long wooden matches, long

Sleep, rough mattresses, gold & hair, golden-haired beauty,
Dark beauty, strewn shoes, apples to apples, so much dust

To dust. *The house ran a touch hot*, is how I'd say it.
Yes, there was two of me. The other was an infernal

Lightweight, so pulped with fear, couldn't stomach
Any of it, like gagging on an aspirin, a rush of spit

To the tongue, a giving of the throat. We spoke
In double cross; it all was very hush-hush. That one

Got gone, second chance she got. Oh, what I can't
Tell you, it's eating me up inside. My stomach burns

With love for her—my eternal bad. I'm asking you
For real: how does anyone know when they're good

& ready? I'm saying, butter don't melt in this mouth—would that
It were true—but it softens, long as I tell it to. I was taken in,

Once. Once upon a time, I was prep. I worked a line. I was
Back of the house. Sugar, there's two kinds: the ones that dull

Their knives in a second drawer & the ones that mise-en-
Place them on a counter. My work, it earns stars. Be my guest,

Check my complexion for a last known address; check my
Oven scorch for downfall. My best evidence jilts me still.

# TRIGGERED, FINGERED

After a time, I took a house. The gun & I
Moved in together. Didn't need its rent, didn't

Need its love neither. Pocketed both. The bullets
Demanded their own room. We signed an ironclad

Lease, sealed the deal. Ran one test finger across all edges &
The lines I left turned to chalk. I craved a touch more rigor

To be honest. The baseboards kept my confidence, left
Me in the dust. The gun had a habit of leaving all

The cabinet doors wide open, hinges greased. The freezer
I held open myself, *an hour badly spent*. Scratch that—

What I wanted was *in*, been told to go get some
Air. Hanging things proved a real chore: gardens,

Cigarette ash, a dress to dry, a dress to rend. The last
Complete thought of a drunk girl pressed as a thumbprint

Into a hot chandelier bulb. A *partial*, so they say.
I shucked each creped evening hour & submitted the silk

As estoppel. The dishwasher, for one, was proper—
Forks up, knives down. Spoons: whatever feels good.

Spooning's just another spec script of good cop, bad cop. Me, I
Hit my mark: far as I'd ever get was *How many times do I have*

*To tell* before the bullets would storm, would storm out,
Slink back, badly spent after dark. The gun knows

From animals (who hold love & hunger), doesn't cotton
To people (who hold water & sighs). It misses whenever

It feels. It feels its own groove. It smokes through its own
Socket. It's smoking. Oh, I've been schooled, you know:

There's safe Latin at the ready for *have the body*, not
So much for *have at the body*. I've been afterschooled.

All my waxed surfaces took on a new spit shine. I saw
Myself here for a good long while, then saw myself

Out. Last dress, best dress. I make no secret of it: I do
Like my sugar, but who said I'd give my teeth for anything.

# AFTER THE GIRL

It's just a chapped lip that won't stop bleeding. Let me
Try that again: strip where the field of the face meets

The woods of the mouth is called *The Invitation*—No,
It's called the *vermilion border*. There are nameless parts

Of the body that are designed to absorb someone else's
Hands. It's just a chipped piece of light that thought

It had my number. It's tough to handle a fishhook &
Not get stuck, the clef of it kissing your hands.

Sometimes, just like anyone else, I see red. In the
Nameless story of *twelve years ago*, a girl takes herself out

Of the picture like pulling something a hound
Shouldn't eat out of its mouth. *A strong female lead.*

Sometimes, just like anyone, I try to wrap my head
Around it. Any number of ways to absorb someone else.

I mean picture it—a girl, her mouth, a brick-red house & you
Without your invitation. Let me try it again. Let the pale

Black lake under my left eye take its name from the girl
Who got hooked, got stuck. It's tough to handle.

Sister, my head aches the way a brick aches when it
First touches mortar. It sounds naughty, the way you

Say it: *The house has me in its backwater embrace.*
That morning, it wasn't the light that hit me.

# GODS GONE WILD

The bees are turning the house to gold, one floorboard at a time. They slip in through the sockets in sixes & sevens, & turn off all the lights as they go. They glow with the gold they bring, their dangling, shimmering limbs like staples pulled bent from the top left corners of reports. The gold spreads like loose pages, skimming the floors as it falls, slipping under sofas, into the bathtub, out through the open windows onto the lawn. *This is what you wanted; this is what you asked for. We were built for this task, is what our golden queen told us, murmuring to us even as she slept in her same corner of our own gold house.* The bees have mixed gold into your lotion, into your furniture polish; they have sifted gold into your coffee & frozen it into the ice cubes you drop in your whiskey. The golden tines of your comb have pulled blonde streaks through your black hair, a look the bees love on you. And there, just under your top left rib, a new queen is turning in her sleep. And when you sigh, you exhale the finest gold silt, softly, softly, soft as your breasts cupped in your own two hands, until it's everywhere & lost, the way a girl goes missing—a sting that smarts, swells, sinks back into the skin, borderless.

IV

# SPOILER

Was born a shamble. Was raised, as many, by a marrow & a follow.
Made first fortune before first word. Had it made. Follow left

The house each morning. Marrow worked to the bone. One
Sinister, one borrow I loved more than my own stalled self;

Early knew for certain one tomorrow I'd make a great ain't. I
Lived from we to we. Tried to save my crumpled singles. Put on

*A bold lip*, pulled firm on my love like hinging down
A set of attic stairs. What a racket. What a small cord

Attaches us. My heart, still the spelling bee I throw each time
On purpose: we had words, then slept like ice in the slit

Of a tucked top sheet. After a spell, sure I slow-ached, sulked
My way awake. Once upon a table: coffee with chicory & make-

Shift bliss. My eyes, bigger than blue-plates—truth, it was almost
Too much to swallow. Took it to go. Clocked myself out. A time

Or two had my lights knocked out, my kneesocks knocked off,
But soft. But still—a ceiling fan, a sill, & a souse who hung

On my every world. No two ways about it; I fell for us, hot &
Mussed as all get out. Took my eastern time across to the Pacific,

Doubled down & doubled back. Put my face in the path
Of another's full-palmed slap—struck by how dumb I was

Struck. Inked myself clear until I was sure as sure was
Numb. Got my house in order but never quite could give up

The drink, the way it confects me, the way I stay spoked
With what wrecks me. Curled myself all the way inside

The inside of our last joke, the punched line we lured
The most, as thicket as our thievery, our ashed plot

Unfallowing me like a neck's own woods toward a choice
Choke of light: I can't imagine, I reckon I can only imagine.

# AIN'T NO PARTY

No kidding! A house killed *my* sister too, I'm telling you. It didn't fall
On top of her, no, but it snipped off a little lock of her each day,
Pickpocketed a small piece of her & replaced it with an exact painted
Replica each day. Then the misdirections, sleights of hand, the way
A best friend is stolen by a new girl in town—one day she has plans
Without you: to pull a liquor bottle out of a cabinet, to crack
An ice tray, to lock a door without you. One day she's giving you
A *dupatta* as a present, & the next she's the *dupatta*, getting caught
In the spokes of a wheel that is actually just her mind, turning
In its blacked-out sleep, like fan blades. But whose house isn't
Out to get them, I s'pose? Whose house doesn't ignite its own
Gas burners once in a while, loosen a board or two at the top of
A staircase? I mean, it kills me, though, the way photos of her begin to
Look so obvious, now that she's gone. Now that she's gone, it's like you
Can see the Springsteen in her eyes, you know? A kind of filter on them
You could find on a smartphone now, called "Missing Girl"
Or "Cold Case" or "How She'll Look When She Shows Up
In That Reoccurring Dream." Her fingers were like the tiny branches
Off an olive tree—twigs, really—not brittle, but no good for sizing
A pour of whiskey, if you get me. And her shoes—there's no easy death
For them, right? Impatient ghosts in & of themselves, bar customers
That don't have to go home but can't stay here. But stay they do,
Chucked off, toppled heels in the hallway. Any good mind would
See them & expect to find her upstairs in bed, a pair of glasses you look
Everywhere for & then find they've been resting on your head
The whole time. I mean, what would you do with *your* sister's shoes?

I've worn them, I admit it—there are times I think they'll never
Come off, that it would take some sort of spell. But I should stop
Now; I should go. Really, it's not my story to tell, I keep telling myself.
I'd shake your hand, but it seems mine is practically made of ice, &
I'd kiss you, full on the lips in a heartbeat, but turns out my mouth will
Put you to sleep. Knock you right out, I tell you what, & you'll wake up in
Some field full of flowers, still in your stilettos, & never want to go home.

# THINGS GO SOUTH

Always trust a red door
On a black Camaro, thighs

Sticking to the vinyl in the June
Sun, pinking up the place.

Here, the apple don't fall
From the tree. Here, whatever you

Find lying on the ground is yours.
A scratch-off waiting to strike. The shade

From a sidelong glance. You're looking at
What happens when a body fights back

Three years after the fact. Three years
After the fact: the sweet morning

Stench of you sweating out last night's liquor
Just by pushing my tongue against the porcelain

Crown glued in my mouth, like hitting a switch.
Every town I leave, I leave on scholarship.

Nothing looks better to me than seeing
Nothing for miles. I can fit everything

I love into this trunk, into my own two arms,
Into my backhanded smile. And this gas station

Bathroom is more than just an American
Notion of the dirtiest place on Earth. It's where

I'll put on my face. I know how to wipe
A scene clean. And then I'm gone, love, like

I was never there. And even if it could hear
You at these speeds, the backseat don't

Care a lick what you have to say. Sweetheart,
I sympathize with the assassin in every story.

# PERSON FAMILIAR WITH THE SITUATION

Not the hell where all your friends await. Not anything *as hell*. Not the rope,
Or hell's rope's end. Not the hell for truants or unchanged engine oil or a hive's

Most recent Queen. Who says we even get another land to tend at all? Fires
To stoke, boulders to cleave. A ferry that practices only one kind of math: a long

Division that reduces all memory of her to the one prayer the prayerless pop
As Ambien: *I did this.* Shhhhh. In here we use our inside eyes, love—haphazard

Rain-tap on the porch roof like the greyhound's cleat nails persisting up
The oak stairs to mark each morning. And you, so fogged away in some scrape

Of city, a hell as serious & routine as a kidney transplant, a handprint
That takes the shape of a bruised fruit. Our history repeals itself. *I wrote*

*Several cards to you but the Post Office was on strike.* The five stages of grief:
Front porch, lemon wedge, fossil fuels, yes, & *yes.* A certain pop tune's

Lick, a shared Southern weather completes the hot-wiring that cranks
Us—you claimed you love the ocean but you only mean her edges.

# IN GROUND WE TRUST

I could be someone who splits her time.

Gospel of Low-Grade Fever. Gospel of You Haven't Touched
Your Drink. I will lie down with you but we won't get up

Together. When the storms get too large, we give them
A name, but not the tornados. When the love gets too

Loud, we swear by it. In four years' time,
These will be the small stories we will tell each

Other, our exculpatory grace, all told. Gospel of So
You Say. My father used to call me *a real pistol.*

I say: *It's not the bullet that kills you, it's the hole.*
When I said *come here*, I meant *come home.*

But there's no house for us to keep, no threshold
We will cross or meet that isn't just the dirt

There is between us, the dust that kicks up, the gusts
That knock us asunder. These will be the small storms

We will wait out for each other, love. *Come here.*

Press both your palms down on my hips, like plunging
Your hands into a full bin of flour. Gospel of The Dust

That Kicks Up. What I mean is: who doesn't want to
Wake up in a different city, just to be able to long

For home, for the way things taste before
They taste like what they're meant to, batter

Licked from a whisk, fingered from the lip
Of the bowl. Stolen.

# WE WILL HAVE WANTED TO HAVE

I said trouble. I meant summer. I can't wait
For *summer* to be over. Just because you're

Sitting tucked up under a bridge doesn't mean
You're in a tunnel, doesn't mean the weather

Won't find you, doesn't mean the train
Villains up the story just because there's tracks

Below you. We'd bought a six-pack, maybe two,
Once. Once we thought it would be the last time.

That would've been a decade ago, maybe
Two. Our currency is drinks. We both pay

For each other, so we owe each other another
Round. It's because I said trouble, isn't it? I meant

Sugar—I can't wait until it gets cold as wedding cake.
The summer will still be there when we're gone.

That time I meant *bridge*, love. We're like bringing
A truck to a train fight. We're in the old Dodge.

Our love is the bench seat. My eyes on you, those two
Scalene door windows, unlatched & angled open.

Just because I'm tucked into you doesn't mean
I want this to be over, doesn't mean we're not

The villains of this story. We'll both weather each
Other, owe each other another summer. At any

One time, there will have been two ways you will find
This could've gone. Your eyes on me, a cold current.

Turn the engine over. Our love is angled
Open. The rain velvets up the story.

# ACKNOWLEDGMENTS

A heat map of your latest reply glows vermilion &

Unfortunate, an orphaned grocery-store orchid. How do I

Give you an out? Love, you poise me, like the small faux jewel

Hot-glued to my lace & wired slip. *I've Been Loving You*

*Too Long* is just one beveled fact like any other. The more

I uncover myself, the less I'm able to use your proper name.

The wake you leave behind is *smirk, wide-eye, B-side, piece of your*

*Sleeve, hand me a glass of anything* & I swear it will become me

To drink it. By which I mean: Sweetheart, I want us to go

Back to the middle of it all. That was the spring I was afraid

Of the wisteria sidling toward my bedroom window

But it was too beautiful to stop. For nearly a whole decade

We all dressed like the teenage boys we longed to be. Back

When I loved my loathsome self the most. Back when

I let you walk; stayed planted in the South myself. You went

To work. What might've turned you to me—your name, another

Fact rooted in my droughted lungs? You woke me. We grew

*Out of it.* The way you first cut off the cold faucet, then wait

Two breaths before cinching off the hot, just to feel how

Things can take a turn so quickly. By which I mean:

*Inchoate.* Like wisteria, we grow closer. The laws we love

The most all sunset as you draw the shades. Listen, set

The turntable's dusty needle gently on my shoulderblade.

You've got me down to my unmentionables.

# THE GIRL NEXT DOOR
# TO THE GIRL NEXT DOOR

Not just somewhere, but here: a girl turns teenage
On the back of a motorbike, its loud lung a bite

Of gristle in the crisp of it all. The ride leaves her
With a small tremor in her right hand—it will not

Leave her, even when the bike leaves her, even when
The teenage leaves her. If she leaves a note, her words

Are tremored like seeing a landscape while your elbows
Are hooked onto somebody from the back. I'm waiting

For her to leave the house. I x up my calendar until
My days are all seeing red. Homewrecker, I am

For fucking real. Guttermouth, I wish she'd ditch me.
My elbows are ditches that collect all her shaky

Punctuation, commas like teeth, knocked loose.
All my days are caught red-handed, stuttering into

Each other's sorry excuse for *I'm so sorry*, & what is a pause
But a way to feel the gaps with our common tongue?

A bite of longing shakes loose like a full tick off
Its host, but the porch party keeps on keeping.

That slammed screen door is no slap—
It's all sucker punch, one bright shiner.

# WHAT SHE DIDN'T LEAVE

Dear friend, dear fearless　　　reader, dear soft spot, dear　　　drummer's
Backstage sweat-soaked T-shirt　　　kiss, dear one　　　sweet　　　world-without

-End, dear *if you*　　　*find this*, dear feckless, damned darkness,　　　dear friendless
Founding pitbull & your shredded　　　fleece bed, dear pitiful　　　scrawl, stained

Spiral-frayed paper-edge, inked back　　　& front, I love you two-
Fold, it's like I was born to　　　ballet-bend back into you,　　　to fold myself　until my

Wrist tendons rise up under　　　my comfortable skin, when you're　　　cornered
Your back's up against *two* walls,　　　your booze is talking, your creatures

Comfort you, I'll walk you　　　through it dear, tend to all　　　the back rent
I owe you,　　　I'll owe you one, *if you're reading*　　　*this*, then you know now,　　　dear

It's like I was born          to break          into other people's houses,          I was born to crawl

Into other people's          beds, *I tried each thing,*          dear fable, only some were flammable &

Lonely, only one could          conjugate me          into my better halves, I've got half

A mind for playing tricks,          I've got an eye          for sparrows, I'm spoiling for

The last word, dear, feed me          my line, oh I will miss our double          features, dear

Movies, your silver          reels          can't frame me anymore, dear movies          your scrim

Is showing, your director's cuts          have burgundy-ed the floor,          love leave the lights

Low, oh I wouldn't          say I'm sorry, exactly          I won't be back until I come back

For you, dear easy way          out, dear          selfless hallway, doorless          fact, faithless

Latch, always protect your own          neck, dear          remember to thank me          for leaving

Just before          all the engineers & artists invented          too many ways to          remember

Too much, dear          chaser, last call,          dear collarbone, you don't have to go home.

# REVERSE: A FAIRY TALE

A pluperfect storm: wolves taken to sporting
Cardigans & Warbys, pinging the forest breeze

For corruption. The witches fondly remembered
As favorite grade-school teachers, formative

But basic. Everyone's mother's working
Third shift; everyone's dad is casually panicked

With *accidentally-salt-instead-of-sugar*. We were supposed to've
Skipped town. We photographed the supper, which was

Too beautiful to serve. Our resting bitch faces stare back
From the improvidence of empty Wedgwood, a presidentless

Clean plate club. Sister, unravel the napkins
From their swans. Un-decant the burgundy &

Cool your burners, dear. Unsneak the bones from their
Low boil. Nothing so unspeakable as an actual wrong

Turn. The wolves give Socratic lectures: *We're impossible*
*To forget, but hard to remember.* Their cold-calls give us

Papercuts, crushes. It's so tempting to turn on
Them, walk back our pebbled position before our

Hour's up, return to the door-to-door, chew on
Our thoughts for a spell, unknock ourselves

Senseless, the way it ever begins, a path &
A girl, a girl swanning right in to some

House that doesn't belong
To her, once upon a tongue.

# NOTES

**Spoiler [It ends with the house in the sky...]**: The line *"hide the pieces, where they may be found"* is, of course, borrowed from John Berryman's "Dream Song 29." The sentence *"it's ok, you're still an animal,"* is a reference to the song "I'm An Animal," by Neko Case.

**Place Like Home**: The line *"I lied when I said I hope I'll see you all again"* is sampled from a poem by Bradley Paul called "How to Deal with the Most Persistent Zombie," from *The Animals All Are Gathering*, University of Pittsburgh Press, 2010.

**Neck Of The Woods**: The "river oversaturated with roses & ash" is the Ganges. The poem is for Jay.

**Spoiler [Where there were fresh brides...]**: The line *"We love a thing we cannot know,"* is borrowed from the poem "Cold Logic," by Beth Bachmann, from her collection *Temper*, University of Pittsburgh Press, 2009.

**The Blueprint**: The phrase *"the sky—the sky—"* is sampled from the William Stafford poem "The Little Girl by the Fence at School," from his collection *Stories That Could Be True*, Harper & Row, 1977.

**Girl Gets Sick Of Rose**: The poem borrows its title, of course, from the Gwendolyn Brooks poem "a song in the front yard," from her *Selected Poems*, 1963.

**We've Been Gone Such A Long Time & We Feel So Messy:** When Dorothy, Toto, The Scarecrow, The Tin Man, & The Cowardly Lion are first permitted entry into the Emerald City, the Cabby (who is also Professor Marvel & the Wizard of Oz) suggests that they "freshen up" before seeing the Wizard. Dorothy thanks him & explains "We've been gone such a long time & we feel so messy."

**White Knuckle**: *"there will be nonsense in it"* is sampled from Lewis Carroll's "All in the golden afternoon," a preface poem introduced in his book *Alice's Adventures in Wonderland*, Macmillan, 1865.

**First Mystery**: The title refers to the first book in the Nancy Drew Mystery Stories, *The Secret of the Old Clock*, Grosset & Dunlap, 1930. The epigraph is a quote from that title. The books were all published under the pen name Carolyn Keene, but written and subsequently revised by different authors. *The Secret of the Old Clock* was originally outlined by Edward Stratemeyer, with the manuscript written by Mildred Wirt Benson. In 1959, it was revised by Harriet Stratemeyer Adams.

**Third Mystery**: The epigraph is a line from the third book in the Nancy Drew Mystery Stories, *The Bungalow Mystery*, Grosset & Dunlap, 1930. The line *"too bad I'm not twins"* is also from the book. Edward Stratemeyer also originally outlined *The Bungalow Mystery*, with the manuscript written by Mildred Wirt Benson. In 1960, it was revised either by Patricia Doll or Harriet Stratemeyer Adams.

**A Girl Keeps Getting Older; The Looking Glass Stays The Same Age** owes inspiration debt to both Lewis Carroll's *Through the Looking-Glass, and What Alice Found There* and a line spoken by the character Wooderson (portrayed by the actor Matthew McConaughey) in the movie *Dazed and Confused*: "That's what I love about these high school girls, man. I get older, they stay the same age."

**Sixth Mystery**: The title refers to the sixth book in the Nancy Drew Mystery Stories, *The Secret of Red Gate Farm*, Grosset & Dunlap, 1931. The book was outlined by Edna Stratemeyer Squier, written by Mildred Witt Benson, and revised in 1961 by Lynn Ealer. The epigraph is also a quote from the book.

**What I Told the Cops**: In U.S. law, the "best evidence rule" holds that when a party seeks to submit the contents of a document as proof, an original document should be used. A facsimile or duplicate of the document can only be used if the original does not exist and/or cannot be obtained.

**Triggered, Fingered**: The phrase "an hour badly spent" is borrowed from the Elizabeth Bishop poem "One Art," from *Geography III*, FSG, 1976. In law, the Latin term *habeas corpus* roughly translates to "have the body." A writ of habeas corpus is used to summon a person before the court to determine issues of unlawful detention.

**Person Familiar With The Situation**: The line *"I wrote several cards to you but the Post Office was on strike"* is a quote from a letter written by writer Breece D'J Pancake on March 25, 1979, when he was living in Charlottesville, VA. The letter is his last known, as Pancake died by suicide on April 8, 1979. The letter is reproduced in *A Room Forever: The Life, Work and Letters of Breece D'J Pancake*, by Thomas E. Douglass, University of Tennessee Press, 2004.

**In Ground We Trust**: The line "it's not the bullet that kills you, it's the hole" is attributed to the artist Laurie Anderson & made its way to me via the poet Charles Wright. The title is a misheard D'Angelo lyric. This poem & "We Will Have Wanted To Have" are both for The Professor.

**What She Didn't Leave**: The phrase *"I tried each thing"* is from the opening line of John Ashbery's "As One Put Drunk into the Packet-Boat," from his collection *Self-Portrait In A Convex Mirror*, Viking Press, 1975.

**Reverse: A Fairy Tale**: The poem owes a debt of stylistic gratitude to Ansel Elkins. The line "impossible to forget, but hard to remember" is borrowed from the Cameron Crowe film *Elizabethtown*. "Warbys" refers to the popular prescription eyeglass frames from Warby Parker.

# Recent Titles from Alice James Books

Alice James Books is committed to publishing books that matter. The press was founded in 1973 in Boston, Massachusetts as a cooperative, wherein authors performed the day-to-day undertakings of the press. This element remains present today, as authors who publish with the press are invited to collaborate closely in the publication process of their work. AJB remains committed to its founders' original feminist mission, while expanding upon the scope to include all voices and poets who might otherwise go unheard. In keeping with its efforts to build equity and increase inclusivity in publishing and the literary arts, AJB seeks out poets whose writing possesses the range, depth, and ability to cultivate empathy in our world and to dynamically push against silence. The press was named for Alice James, sister to William and Henry, whose extraordinary gift for writing went unrecognized during her lifetime.

Designed by

PAMELA A. CONSOLAZIO

*Spark design*

PRINTED BY MCNAUGHTON & GUNN